Steam Ramble
NUMBER 1
SOUTH
and WEST

Steam Ramble
NUMBER 1
SOUTH
and WEST

Steam Ramble
NUMBER 1
SOUTH
and WEST

M. Pope

LONDON
IAN ALLAN LTD

First published 1976

ISBN 0 7110 0729 2

© M. Pope

Published by Ian Allan Ltd, Shepperton, Surrey,
and printed in the United Kingdom by
Ian Allan Printing Ltd.

Title page: 'On the rattler': Class U 2-6-0 No 31799 on the Reading-Redhill line,
seen soon after leaving Shalford, bound for Guildford and Reading in 1964.

This page: 'West Country' Pacific No 34100 *Appledore* heads the down 'Golden
Arrow' past Folkestone Warren in 1961.

Introduction

A vast number of railway photographic albums have appeared over the last few years, embracing a variety of subjects from specific areas of the British Isles to individual railway companies or regions. I have not set out to specialise in any particular field. As the title implies, this book is a gentle browse in the kaleidoscope of BR steam scenes over a period of approximately ten years, enthusing over the varied happenings they recall. To coin a well-worn phrase, "every picture tells a story", for behind every photograph lies a wealth of anecdotes, fun and even tragedy, plus always the inevitable British weather.

Basically photography began for me in the mid-1950s, commencing with sporadic trips on a bicycle from Ealing to such vantage points as Southall footbridge, West Ealing, Willesden and Kenton. Owing to a lack of ready cash — yes, we had cash flow problems then too — such limited ventures were the rule for a considerable time. In those days even a roll of black and white film was rather an expensive luxury and an item not to be consumed too rapidly. After a while my friends and I did become more venturesome and we found ourselves cycling to more distant locations, like the three "Ss" — Saunderton, Sonning and Sole Street — many miles away. These were epic excursions that I wouldn't dream of repeating now, but what great enjoyment it all was.

As finances improved I found myself making longer and more exciting visits to various previously unattainable locations, over the length and breadth of the country. Often these trips were made by excursion trains. The BR Bank Holiday Overnight Specials to such places as Plymouth, York and Leeds were very advantageous. These outings culminated in whole weeks at the very comfortable "Greyhound" at Shap — complete with its Duttons of Blackburn of course!

One of the greatest problems of this era was to try to get one's priorities right. I think only a few people succeeded here. Every week brought masses of locomotive withdrawals from different areas, often including last of classes, coupled with closures of numerous branch and cross-country lines. Being wise after the event, as we always are, the ideal situation would have been to have captured on film all these impending withdrawals and closures as or even before they happened, but unfortunately I seem for various reasons to have missed out on a lot of them. Still, as some form of consolation during this busy era, even with all the time in the world one just wouldn't have been able to cover every interesting steam happening in every part of the country.

Richmond, Surrey.   Mike Pope

Right: "Front ends" at Waterloo: rebuilt 'Merchant Navy' Pacific No 35028 *Clan Line* and a 4COR Portsmouth set in 1965. The 'MN' is now preserved.

Below: The down 'Bournemouth Belle' in Farnborough cutting headed by rebuilt 'Merchant Navy' Pacific No 35028 *Clan Line* on a Sunday in 1960. It was usual during this period for the 'Belle' not to carry a headboard on Sundays.

Far right: 'Deepcut': unrebuilt 'West Country' Pacific No 34092 *City of Wells* streaks through with an up train in 1964.

Below right: Diversion: whilst the Bournemouth main line was being electrified, many of the Sunday main-line trains were diverted either via Alton to Winchester or by the Portsmouth line via Havant along the coast. Here rebuilt 'West Country' Pacific No 34101 *Hartland* plods up the climb to Tunnel Hill, between Brookwood and Ash Vale, with a down train in 1966. Pirbright Junction is in the far distance.

Left: The down afternoon empty milk tanks from Vauxhall to the West of England being hauled through Deepcut by BR Standard Class 5 4-6-0 No 73114 *Etarre* in 1964.

Below: Class H16 4-6-2T No 30517 gleams in Wimbledon Yard, prior to working a railtour in the suburban area in 1962.

Right: Farnborough and a Salisbury-Waterloo afternoon stopping train with 'King Arthur' 4-6-0 No 30451 *Sir Lamorak* in charge in 1961.

Below right: Winchfield: rebuilt 'West Country' 4-6-2 No 34040 *Crewkerne* at speed with a down Bournemouth line train in 1966.

Left: Two Class 0298 2-4-0 WTs from the Wenford Bridge china clay line in Cornwall were used on an enthusiasts' railtour of the Waterloo suburban lines in December 1962. In frosty conditions, Nos 30585 and 30587 head down the relief line through Raynes Park.

Right: BR Class 3 2-6-2T No 82006 in green livery busies itself on shunting duties at Waterloo in 1965.

Below: Wimbledon flyover and rebuilt 'West Country' Pacific No 34017 *Ilfracombe* rolls over with an up train in 1965.

On the 'Rattler' again — and this time with a 'foreigner' in the form of WR 4-6-0 No 7808 *Cookham Manor* on a through train from Eastbourne to Tyseley, seen in 1962 between North Camp and Farnborough North en route to Reading where it will join the Western main line. (*Cookham Manor* is now preserved at Didcot.)

Autumn sunshine near Pirbright Junction and Class U 2-6-0 No 31627 hurrying a late afternoon freight train westward in October 1964.

Above: Class H 0-4-4T No 31521 makes a rare appearance in Victoria station to work an enthusiasts' special over lines and branches in the South London area in April 1958.

Right: London Bridge station viewed from the carriage window of the down 1.10pm Charing Cross-Ramsgate train, unusually double-headed on this occasion by Class D1 4-4-0 No 31739 and unrebuilt 'Battle of Britain' 4-6-2 No 34083 *605 Squadron.*

Above right: The 'Kentish Belle' leaving Victoria for the Kent Coast resorts in 1957, hauled by 'Schools' Class 4-4-0 No 30916 *Whitgift.*

Far right: The down 'Golden Arrow' approaching Knockholt as it rushes towards Dover in 1959, with unrebuilt 'Battle of Britain' Pacific No 34089 *602 Squadron* in charge.

The 'Arrow' again, this time during the last few weeks of steam operation in 1961, seen leaving Victoria hauled by rebuilt 'West Country' Pacific No 34100 *Appledore*.

Folkestone Junction, with 'Schools' Class 4-4-0 No 30930 *Radley* approaching at speed on a down excursion in 1961.

Left: Unrebuilt 'Battle of Britain' Pacific No 34073 *249 Squadron* heads through Folkestone Junction with an up boat train from Dover in 1961.

Below: Folkestone Harbour in March 1961: by this time ex-GW pannier tanks had replaced the old R1 tanks, used for so many years. Here Nos 4601 and 4616 labour away from the Harbour with an up boat train, helped by another pannier in the rear.

Right: Folkestone Warren: Class D1 4-4-0 No 31739 heads the down 7.24am train from Holborn Viaduct to Ramsgate through the Warren, just prior to electrification in 1961.

Below right: Folkestone Harbour: an up boat train being helped by a ex-GW pannier tank No 4610 in 1961.

Left: Dover Marine in December 1957 and Class O1 0-6-0 No 31258 shunting vans.

Top: Class Q1 0-6-0 No 33035 hurries through Folkestone Warren with a stopping train to Dover in 1961.

Above: The last few weeks in 1961 of the steam-hauled 'Golden Arrow', seen here emerging from Shakespeare Tunnel, Dover, hauled by rebuilt 'West Country' Pacific No 34100 *Appledore.*

Left: Three Bridges in 1963, with Class H 0-4-4T No 31518 veering away from the main line on a branch train for East Grinstead.

Above: The Guildford-Horsham line: a down enthusiasts' special train leaving Baynards, headed by Class USA 0-6-0T No 30064 in October 1964. (This locomotive is now preserved on the Bluebell Railway.)

Below: Paddock Wood in 1961: Class H 0-4-4T No 31500 blasts away with a local train to Maidstone. On the left is the interesting Paddock Wood signalbox, whence the Hawkhurst branch used to sweep through the 'Kitchen' to its destination.

Left: Class K 2-6-0 No 32353 approaches Partridge Green in fading sunlight in October 1962 with an enthusiasts' special returning to London over the Steyning line.

Below: Class D1 4-4-0 No 31739 and Class E1 4-4-0 No 31067 head a down ramblers' excursion from Victoria to Hawkhurst in May 1961, just before the closure of the Hawkhurst branch; they are seen near Edenbridge.

Right: Paddock Wood again, in March 1961; Class N 2-6-0 No 31404 is leaving the station with a down stopping train. The Hawkhurst branch diverges to the left.

Below right: Another enthusiasts' special in the South in October 1962, heading through Falmer on an up gradient en route from Brighton to Seaford, hauled by Class A1X 0-6-0T No 32636 and Class E6 0-6-2T No 32418.

Above left: The last train over the Horsham-Guildford line in June 1965 was an enthusiasts' special, seen here waiting to leave Baynards for Guildford and London. Two Class Q1 0-6-0s, Nos 33027 and 33006, provide ample power.

Left: Eastbourne Shed was host in 1962 to two unfamiliar faces; Class M7 0-4-4T No 30055 and the restored Class T9 4-4-0 No 120 which had worked in on an enthusiasts' special.

Above: The Lymington branch in 1964: a Brockenhurst train crossing the creek between Lymington Pier and Town stations, headed by Class M7 0-4-4T No 30053 (now preserved in the USA).

Right: The last survivor of Class C14, 0-4-4T No 77S, finished its days as Eastleigh Works/shed pilot in 1959.

Above: A special enthusiasts' train to Bulford Camp in 1963, seen diverging from the main line near the site of Amesbury Junction behind Class Q1 0-6-0 No 33039.

Left: Restored Class T9 No 120 runs light engine past Allington signalbox at the site of the former Amesbury Junction, on its way to Salisbury to pick up an enthusiasts' special in 1963.

Right: Storm clouds are brewing at Basingstoke in 1966 as the last rays of sun highlight grubby rebuilt 'Battle of Britain' Pacific No 34056 *Croydon*, seen slipping on departure with a down Bournemouth line train.

Far left: On a frosty morning in 1965 rebuilt 'Merchant Navy' Pacific No 35019 *French Line CGT* hammers towards Basingstoke with a down Bournemouth line train.

Left: Salisbury in the summer of 1960: unrebuilt 'Battle of Britain' Pacific No 34049 *Anti-Aircraft Command* leaves with an up train and No 34104 *Bere Alston* waits to follow.

Below: Confrontation at Bournemouth shed in 1965 between two rebuilt Bulleid Pacifics: on the left 'West Country' No 34008 *Padstow* and on the right 'Merchant Navy' No 35028 *Clan Line.*

Left: BR Standard Class 5 4-6-0 No 73113 *Lyonesse* rushes along the Bournemouth road past Battledown flyover near Worting Junction with a down train in 1960.

Below: Eastleigh shed in 1962, with 'Lord Nelson' 4-6-0 No 30857 *Lord Howe* in evidence.

Right: A stranger at Basingstoke in 1965 is an LM Class 5 4-6-0 making a rousing start after a water stop with a down troop train off the Reading line.

Left: Rebuilt 'Merchant Navy' Pacific No 35026 *Lamport & Holt Line* is eased slightly on the approach to Worting Junction with the up 'Bournemouth Belle' in 1965.

Below: Unusual power for the up 'Bournemouth Belle' in October 1966 is grimy BR standard Class 5 4-6-0 No 73118, seen leaving Bournemouth Central for Waterloo.

Right: An up train passing Lymington Junction in 1964, hauled by unrebuilt 'West Country' Pacific No 34105 *Swanage.*

Below right: Canute Road, Southampton: restored Class T9 4-4-0 No 120 crosses light engine after working an enthusiasts' special to the Ocean Liner Terminal in 1963.

View from Corfe Castle in 1965, showing part of Corfe village and a BR Standard Class 4 2-6-4T leaving the station on a Swanage-Wareham branch train.

As mentioned earlier, certain trains were diverted whilst the Bournemouth main line was being electrified. Here in 1965, BR standard Class 5 4-6-0 No 73171 slogs up the 1 in 80 gradient between Witley and Haslemere, on the Portsmouth line, with a down train.

Above: Southampton Central: rebuilt 'Merchant Navy' Pacific No 35030 *Elder Dempster Lines* leaves with a down Weymouth train.

Right: Battledown flyover, near Worting Junction: Class N15 4-6-0 No 30453 *King Arthur* heads westwards with a stopping train to Salisbury in April 1960.

Far right: Dorchester South station in 1967: rebuilt 'West Country' Pacific No 34008 *Padstow* has a blow-up before departing for Waterloo. The train has just completed the curious movement required by up trains at Dorchester in steam days, whereby they ran through the station via the line in the foreground and then set back to reach the up platform.

Right: Upwey Bank out of Weymouth in 1966: a return enthusiasts' special strides steadily up the incline, headed by BR standard Class 4 2-6-0 No 76026 and standard Class 5 4-6-0 No 73029.

Below: Between the tunnels at Upwey in 1965: rebuilt 'West Country' Pacific No 34009 *Lyme Regis* with an up Waterloo train.

Below right: Wallers Ash Tunnel, between Winchester and Micheldever: unrebuilt 'West Country' Pacific No 34023 *Blackmore Vale* emerges cautiously with the up Saturday Redbridge-Wimbledon rails train in 1966. (No 34023 is now preserved on the Bluebell line.)

Above: In 1960 'King Arthur' 4-6-0 No 30796 *Sir Dodinas Le Savage* rounds the curve towards Battledown flyover on the West of England line with an up evening stopping train from Salisbury to Waterloo.

Left: Another Sunday train diverted due to main line electrification work: unrebuilt 'Battle of Britain' Pacific No 34064 *Fighter Command*, fitted experimentally with Giesl ejector, heads a down train at speed through Froyle en route to Alton and Winchester in 1966.

Above right: Rebuilt 'Battle of Britain' Pacific No 34059 *Sir Archibald Sinclair* runs downhill out of Upwey tunnel with the Weymouth portion of a train from Waterloo in 1965.

Right: Southampton Central: unrebuilt 'West Country' Pacific 34102 *Lapford* threads the station carefully and is opened up just before the tunnel with the up Redbridge-Wimbledon rails train in 1967.

Left: The down 'Bournemouth Belle', diverted via Alton and the Winchester line in 1966, is here climbing the steep gradient to Medstead. The pilot locomotive is BR Class 3 2-6-0 No 77014 — a very rare visitor that appeared on the Southern for a few months towards the end of steam traction — and the train locomotive unrebuilt 'West Country' Pacific No 34102 *Lapford.*

Below: Another double-headed diversion in 1966 photographed soon after leaving Alton and taking the mid-Hants line to Winchester, the other line being the old Meon Valley line; the lines separated just beyond this location, at Butts Junction. The train is double-headed by a BR Class 5 4-6-0 and rebuilt 'Battle of Britain' Pacific No 34077 *603 Squadron.*

Right: Rebuilt 'Merchant Navy' Pacific No 35008 *Orient Line* vigorously attacks Medstead Bank between Alton and Winchester with a diverted down train in 1966.

Below right: In the New Forest area: unrebuilt 'West Country' Pacific No 34006 *Bude* heads an up train across the moor between Sway and Brockenhurst in 1966.

Right: The Isle of Wight: Class O2 0-4-4T No 22 *Brading* emerges from the tunnel whilst running round at Ventnor, around 1962.

Below: Wroxall, Isle of Wight: Class O2 0-4-4T No 22 *Brading* about to leave with a Ventnor train in 1964.

Far right: A Princes Risborough to Marylebone stopping train on the GW/GC Joint section near Seer Green in 1960, hauled by LMS Class 4 2-6-4T No 42230.

Below right: The Oxford to Princes Risborough branch service in 1962, seen here on the approach to Risborough headed by WR 2-6-2T No 6106. The line diverging to the left is the Watlington branch: the two branches were separate lines out of Risborough. (No 6106 is now preserved at Didcot.)

Far left: Interior of Old Oak Common shed in 1961, with two of the 0-6-0 condensing tanks built for working over the London Transport Widened Lines to Smithfield, Nos 9700 and 9706.

Above: WR 2-8-0 No 4702 in Old Oak Common shed.

Below: Two days before Christmas 1961 and in bitter cold, 'Castle' 4-6-0 No 5078 *Beaufort*, having made a special stop at Southall to pick up, is blasting away westwards with a heavier than usual pre-Christmas load.

Above: These large, strong, healthy WR 47XX 2-8-0s were sometimes known as ''nightbirds''. No 4707 is passing Iver with a down freight train.

Right: The down Sunday afternoon van train from Paddington was invariably an ex-works locomotive running-in turn. 'King' 4-6-0 No 6027 *King Richard I* heads the vans through West Ealing in 1961.

Above right: The famous 4-4-0 No 3440 *City of Truro* poses at Kensington Olympia, in front of the Westward Television exhibition train that stayed there for several days before commencing a tour of the West Country in February 1961.

Far right: WR 4-6-0 No 1002 *County of Berks* heads a down Christmas parcels van train past Southall gasworks in 1961.

Far left: Kensington Olympia in July 1965. An enthusiasts' railtour arrives, hauled by immaculate green-lined out Ivatt Class 2 2-6-0 No 46509 from Willesden shed.

Left: The front end of No 7029 *Clun Castle* when allocated to Old Oak Common shed in 1962.

Below left: Double-chimney 'Castle' 4-6-0 No 5057 *Earl Waldegrave* barks away from a signal check at Iver with the down 3.00pm milk empties from West Ealing in 1963.

Below: Often Southall shed would collect a number of freight locomotives that had worked up during the week and return them to their respective depots as a complete train. Here four 2-8-0s, Nos 3822, 2807, 3827 and 3837, push out from the shed to reverse and gain the down relief line in October 1961.

Left: Ex-works 4-6-0 No 6868 *Penhros Grange* rounds the Greenford loop at West Ealing with an up freight train in 1963.

Right: The down 2.55pm train to South Wales was often double-headed on Saturdays; here 4-6-0s No 1024 *County of Pembroke* and 5050 *Earl of St Germans* accelerate through Ealing Broadway in 1961.

Below: 'Castle' 4-6-0 No 5057 *Earl Waldegrave* passes Southall shed with the down 6.35pm Paddington-Swindon train in 1961.

Left: A rare visitor to Southall shed in 1965 was Class A4 4-6-2 No 60007 *Sir Nigel Gresley*, on shed for servicing after working an enthusiasts' special to Paddington (see facing page).

Right: Another rare working on the Western was by 4-6-0 No 30850 *Lord Nelson*, borrowed from the Southern in June 1962 to work an enthusiasts' special from Paddington to Swindon. It is seen here passing Southall at speed — in fact it was probably the fastest down train I had seen here in years. The local fire brigade took some while to extinguish the several bank fires it started.

Below: Stranger on the Birmingham line: Class A4 4-6-2 No 60007 *Sir Nigel Gresley* is getting away from High Wycombe after a water stop there with an enthusiasts' special to Paddington in 1965.

Left: Oxford shed in 1957: WR 4-6-0 No 5026 *Criccieth Castle* gets the full works before setting back to the station and taking over a northbound train.

Below: When first fully restored WR 4-6-0 No 4079 *Pendennis Castle* was allocated to Southall shed — where it is seen in August, 1965 — and worked the evening Slough-Reading freight train and return as a running-in turn.

Right: Ashendon Junction signalbox: 'King' 4-6-0 No 6014 *King Henry VII* approaches at speed with a down Birmingham line train in 1961.

Below right: WR 2-6-2T No 6129 leaving Oxford with an up stopping train in 1962.

Above: Down freight train at 'Lands End' near Woodley in 1963, headed by 2-8-0 No 2891. Twyford station is in the far distance.

Left: The remains of that long bitter winter of 1962/3 are still in evidence in Sonning cutting in March 1963 as 4-6-0 No 1002 *County of Berks* heads the down 11.45am train from Paddington under the A4 road bridge.

Above right: WR 4-6-0 No 6001 *King Edward VII* heads the down 6.10pm Paddington-Birkenhead train between Saunderton and Princes Risborough in May, 1960. The down line appears as a single line here, whilst the up line is on the left in a deep cutting.

Right: Still showing signs of the bitter winter of 1962/3, WR 4-6-0 No 5922 *Caxton Hall* heads an up freight train through Sonning cutting in March 1963.

Left: WR 4-6-0 No 5001 *Llandovery Castle* heads the Sunday 1.10pm Paddington-Birmingham train through Greenford in September 1962.

Below left: WR 4-6-0 *King James I* on the turntable at Newbury racecourse after arriving there with a race sepcial in October 1962.

Right: WR 4-6-0 No 6022 *King Edward III* skims over Ruislip troughs and takes just a little refreshment, heading an up train from Wolverhampton and Birmingham in September 1962.

Below: Newbury racecourse, October 1962: the three race specials from Paddington were all 'King'-hauled that day, by Nos 6000, 6005 and 6011. Here Nos 6000 *King George V* and 6005 *King George II* have been turned and wait patiently until the racing is over so that they can return to Paddington.

Above: The down Sunday 4.10pm train on the Birmingham line near Seer Green Halt (GW/GC Joint section), headed by WR 4-6-0 No 7026 *Tenby Castle* of Stafford Road shed in September 1962.

Right: Swindon works May 1960: WR 4-6-0 No 5037 *Monmouth Castle* is undergoing major overhaul.

Far right: WR 4-6-0 No 6016 *King Edward V* hurries the up 'Cambrian Coast Express' through the deep cutting between Princes Risborough and Saunderton in July 1961.

Above left: The Didcot, Newbury & Southampton line in February 1960. A train from Newbury to Eastleigh enters the DN&S from the main line at Enborne Junction near Newbury, headed by Mogul No 6313.

Left: The M&SWJR in August 1961: Southern Class N 2-6-0 No 31844 on a stopping train to Andover passes Grafton Junction box soon after leaving Savernake. The GW main line can be seen in the background, running left to right.

Above: A DN&S train bound for Newbury, with WR 0-6-0 No 2240 in charge, approaches Highclere in February 1960.

Right: The DN&S line: the last day of passenger service, 5 March 1960 — "Bessie", the station lady of Burghclere.

WR 4-6-0 No 6000 *King George V* in Swindon running shed roundhouse, highlighted by afternoon sun in October 1962.

Swindon shed, 1963, with No 1013 *County of Dorset* in the roundhouse; at this time only six 'Counties' remained, all allocated to Swindon.

Left: The Gloucester-Chalford Auto in April 1962: WR 0-4-2T No 1473 is leaving Ham Mill Halt with a Sunday train to Chalford.

Below: The Chalford Auto again, this time in June 1963, with 0-4-2T No 1424 climbing through the valley towards Brimscombe.

Right: View from the front passenger compartment of a dmu travelling in the up direction near Great Bedwyn, as WR 4-6-0 No 5945 *Leckhampton Hall* approaches with a down freight train in September 1962. The Kennet & Avon canal is on the right.

Left: A down West of England summer Saturday extra train pounds past the Kennet & Avon Canal Co's pumping station at Crofton, towards the summit at Savernake in 1962, headed by WR 'Castle' 4-6-0 No 5060 *Earl of Berkeley.*

Below: A Bristol-Derby train leaving Gloucester Eastgate in 1963, headed by 'Jubilee' 4-6-0 No 45564 *New South Wales.*

Right: A visitor to Swindon shed in March 1963 was Class A4 Pacific No 60022 *Mallard*, having arrived with an enthusiasts' special. The gallant shed staff, undeterred by pouring rain, brought out No 6000 *King George V* to be photographed alongside.

Below: More strange goings-on at Swindon shed in May 1964, when Stanier Pacific No 46251 *City of Nottingham* arrived from the East Midlands via the Great Central line with an enthusiasts' special. The WR 4-6-0 on the left, No 7022 *Hereford Castle* in 'bulled-up' condition, was standby locomotive for the last leg of the Ian Allan high-speed railtour from Plymouth to Paddington on the same day. Also in evidence was WR No 7929 *Wyke Hall*.

Left: A foggy day in Swindon town in December 1963 as yet a further strange face appears on shed, this time BR Class 6 Pacific No 72006 *Clan Mackenzie*, having worked an enthusiasts' special from Paddington in the murk.

Top: Swindon station in May 1960: WR 2-8-0 No 4707 waits for the right away on the centre road with an up van train.

Above: An unusual type to undergo repair on Swindon shed in March 1963 was this Somerset & Dorset 2-8-0.

Right: The Somerset & Dorset line in 1964: S&D 2-8-0 No 53807 and a Class 4F 0-6-0 climb the gradient near Shepton Mallet with an enthusiasts' special from Bournemouth to Bath.

Left: Sunday milk train from Bailey Gate to Templecombe consisting of WR pannier 0-6-0T No 4634, a milk tank and a brake van, leaving Bailey Gate in March 1964. The milk depot is on the left.

Below: The Sunday milk empties leaving Templecombe for Bailey Gate in October 1963, with Class 2 2-6-2T No 41242 in charge. The connecting line from the S&D to Templecombe main line is on the left.

Right: A wet Saturday morning on the S&D at Wincanton in 1964. The morning Bath-Bournemouth stopping train is unusually double-headed by 2-8-0 No 53807 and a Class 4F 0-6-0. Both locomotives were worked to Bournemouth on this train to stay overnight ready for a railtour on the Sunday (see page 77).

Below right: One of the S&D line's summer Saturday services was the Cleethorpes-Sidmouth through train, seen emerging from Chilcompton tunnel in August 1962 behind a BR Standard Class 4 4-6-0 and an LMS Class 4F 0-6-0.

Above: Two unrebuilt Bulleid Pacifics, Nos 34006 *Bude* and 34057 *Biggin Hill*, grace the Somerset & Dorset line with an enthusiasts' special on the last day of service, March 5, 1966. They are seen here between Chilcompton and Masbury.

Left: Unrebuilt 'Battle of Britain' Pacific No 34057 *Biggin Hill* tackles the 1 in 50 climb to Evershot tunnel, between Yeovil and Dorchester, with a ten-coach public excursion from Salisbury to Weymouth, in 1964. The train is banked in rear by a BR Class 3 2-6-2T.

Left: WR 0-4-2T No 1451 works an auto-train from Yeovil Junction to Yeovil Town in October 1963.

Below: A Yeovil-Taunton train on the down main line between Langport and Athelney, headed by BR Class 3 2-6-2T No 82008 in October 1963.

Right: The Yeovil-Taunton line again, with WR 2-6-2T No 4569 on a Taunton train near Thorney Halt in 1964.

Below right: A local train from Highbridge to Evercreech Junction, on the S&D, approaching Pylle in October 1963 headed by Class 2 2-6-2T No 41296.

Right: A down West of England train, hauled by rebuilt 'Merchant Navy' Pacific No 35024 *East Asiatic Company*, hurries through the closed station of Sutton Bingham, west of Yeovil, in 1964.

Below: The Lyme Regis branch in 1965: Class 2 2-6-2T No 41216, having taken over from the old Class 0415 4-4-2Ts, is seen climbing the bank soon after crossing Cannington Viaduct with a train for Lyme Regis.

Below right: A Sunday morning stopping train from Exeter to Yeovil Town seen leaving Yeovil Junction and taking the town line in October 1963. Ample power is supplied by unrebuilt 'Battle of Britain' Pacific No 34070 *Manston.*

Top: Plymouth North Road in 1960: on the right WR 'Castle' 4-6-0 No 5084 *Reading Abbey*, having arrived with an excursion from Paddington; on the left, rebuilt SR 'Battle of Britain' Pacific No 34058 *Sir Frederick Pile* waits for the road with an Exeter and Waterloo train.

Above: An up Waterloo express soon after leaving Yeovil Junction in 1964 with rebuilt 'Merchant Navy' Pacific No 35012 *United States Lines* making a very lively getaway.

Right: Visitor to the Southern: Class A2 Pacific No 60532 *Blue Peter* ascends Hewish Bank soon after passing Crewkerne with an enthusiasts' special from Waterloo to Exeter in August 1966.

Left: Just what I needed! A situation that must surely have been experienced by every steam railway photographer at some time or another: rebuilt 'Battle of Britain' Pacific No 34062 *17 Squadron*, heading a down train somewhere west of Salisbury in 1964, leaves a smokescreen through burning just coal dust in a strong southerly wind.

Below left: The Seaton branch in 1965 with Western motive power: 0-4-2T No 1442 leaves Colyton station with a Seaton Junction-Seaton train.

Right: WR 4-6-0 No 5098 *Clifford Castle* takes the Western road at Cowley Bridge near Exeter with an up fruit and vegetable extra train in June 1963. The Southern line to the West diverges in the foreground.

Below: Quite often on summer Saturdays the huge WR 47XX 2-8-0s were rostered for relief workings to the West Country. No 4703 is seen here rolling into Exeter St. Davids with a relief Paddington-Kingswear train in July 1960.

Left: Everything around echoes to the brisk bark as double-chimney 4-6-0 No 5098 *Clifford Castle* steadily climbs the west side of Dainton Bank with an up loaded milk train in August 1961.

Top: WR 4-6-0 No 7022 *Hereford Castle* pilots 'Warship' diesel-hydraulic No D821 *Greyhound* out of Par with a local train to Newquay on a summer Saturday in July 1960. This strange form of double-heading was a means of conveying main-line locomotives to Newquay to work return summer Saturday holiday trains.

Above: The down Sunday 'Torbay Express' coasts along the sea wall near Dawlish in June 1961, behind WR 4-6-0 No 5003 *Lulworth Castle*. It was usual at this period of time for named trains not to carry headboards on Sundays.

Above Left: Night time at Newton Abbot: WR 4-6-0 No 4905 *Barton Hall* has arrived with a stopping train from Exeter in July 1960.

Left: WR 4-6-0 No 6849 *Walton Grange* eases out of Dainton Tunnel and begins to roll down the west side of the summit with a down train in 1961.

Above: WR 2-6-2T No 4570 rounds a curve near Carbis Bay with a St Erth-St Ives train in July 1960.

Right: WR 2-6-2Ts Nos 4593 and 5537 pass through Shepherds station in the early morning with empty stock from Newquay to Perranporth, to form part of the up summer Saturday Perranporth-Paddington through train in July 1960.

Left: China clay branch train: WR 0-6-0PTs Nos 1664 and 1626 stop for water on the return trip up the Carbean branch with a loaded clay train from Carbean to Goonbarrow Junction in July 1960.

Below: Cornish china clay traffic: at Goonbarrow Junction, on the Par-Newquay line in July 1960, a large train of china clay empties destined for Meledor Mill is hustled along behind an odd combination of WR 2-8-0T No 4273 and 2-6-2T No 4559.

Right: China clay empties from Wadebridge to Wenford hauled by Class 0298 2-4-0WT No 30587, seen diverging from the Bodmin line to the Wenford branch in 1960. The last three locomotives of this class lingered at Wadebridge for many years, retained there to work mainly the Wenford Bridge china clay branch and also to act as the Wadebridge station pilot; they were occasionally let loose on the local school train to Bodmin North.

Below right: St Blazey shed in 1960, showing two 'Manors', Nos 7806 *Cockington Manor* and 7816 *Frilsham Manor*, plus 2-6-2T No 5193.

The last steam train from Plymouth to Penzance, an enthusiasts' special on 3 May, 1964, seen crossing the Royal Albert Bridge, Saltash, hauled by unrebuilt 'West Country' Pacific No 34002 *Salisbury*.